SoHo
New York

SoHo New York

STEVE KAHN

INTRODUCTION BY ERIC NASH

Rizzoli
NEW YORK

ACKNOWLEDGMENTS

Thanks to: Bevan Davies, Sara Beth Hobel and David
Wallace for their help and guidance; Henry Buhl and the
SoHo Partnership for its support; Robin and Zoe for their
patience and understanding; Joe Campagna and ICON
Digital Photography (NYC) for image editing. And a special
thanks to Peter Deutsch, without whose interest, generosity,
and encouragement there might not have been a book at all.

For the memory of Robert Overby – friend and mentor.

First published in the United States of America in 1999 by
Rizzoli International Publications, Inc.
300 Park Avenue South
New York, NY 10010

ISBN 0-8478-2156-0
LC 99-70708

Designed by Peter Deutsch of Deutsch Design, Inc.

Printed in Italy

TABLE OF CONTENTS

Introduction

According to Webster's, a palimpsest is a page that has been written upon many times, so that imperfect traces of earlier texts remain. SoHo is a palimpsest upon which the history of New York City has been written. Today it is the American equivalent of Milan's fashionable Via della Spiga or the Via de' Tornabuoni in Florence: the buzz on the street is as much about fashion, commerce, and fine food as about fine art. In the late 1980s the bubble of SoHo's art world—epitomized by such artists as Julian Schnabel, David Salle, Jean-Michel Basquiat, Keith Haring, and Jeff Koons—burst, and spaces where prominent galleries once showed their work have since been transformed into fashion boutiques.

35 Wooster Street

Art may no longer be the engine that drives SoHo, but it is still a vital presence, lending cachet to a glittering neighborhood of bistros and boutiques that set trends for the global village. The streets provide a parade of characters at all hours: people wearing more black than a New Orleans funeral procession, women in scantier outfits than the mannequins in the boutique windows, baby strollers, mountain bikes, exotic dogs, and all the raucous symbols of America at play, from flashy chrome Harley-Davidsons to convertibles with stereos turned up to the sound-level of a jet taking off. Just listening to the conversations in the crowds reveals an environment as polyglot as the United Nations.

Long-time residents can remember when SoHo was a down-at-the-heels neighborhood of lofts used for light industrial purposes, where you could find the most extraordinary trash in the streets at night—buttons, ribbons, trimmings, doll parts, packing materials—the residue of marginal industries left behind by modernization. The neighborhood was filled with the sounds and smells of industry: on weekdays, the banging of trucks being loaded and, at night, the sweet aroma of baking bread wafting from the Bakery Building at 130 Prince Street. Today, amidst the models catwalking by on clunky-soled shoes, you can still see workers trundling bolts of cloth.

42 Greene Street

Artists in noticeable numbers first moved into the area in the late 1960s. Early artists resident in SoHo included Donald Judd, Alex Katz, Chuck Close, and Ronald Bladen. They found the combination of low rents, high ceilings, spaces filled with light from tall windows, and sturdy floors to be ideal for producing their over-size works. In defiance of city codes, the artists also set up their homes in the buildings, which were zoned for industrial use only. The artists' presence had little impact on the physical aspect of the neighborhood, except to bring crowds of uptowners trooping up the steep loft stairwells to look at their shows. Back then, there were few grocery stores in the area, and, to eat out, only the restaurants of Chinatown and the Lower East Side (old-timers will fondly remember Food, the cooperative health food restaurant at the corner of Prince and Wooster).

SoHo's very existence had been threatened by the plans of New York's construction czar Robert Moses, who transformed the face of the city as thoroughly, if not as elegantly, as Baron Hauss-mann changed Paris. Moses had sought to tear down the aging and unprofitable cast-iron buildings to make way for a Lower Manhat-tan Expressway, which would have cut through the heart of SoHo on Broome Street to link the Holland Tunnel with the Williams-burg and Manhattan Bridges. Fortunately, the proposal, which had been in the works since before World War II, was stopped when the artists joined forces with a group of preservationists including Jane Jacobs, James Marston Fitch, and Margot Gayle, who founded the Friends of Cast-Iron Architecture in 1970.

In 1973 SoHo was designated a historic district, described as the largest and finest concentration of cast-iron architecture in the world. It owes this status to a combination of intense early development and subsequent benign neglect. Though first invented in England, cast-iron was primarily developed in America during the second half of the nineteenth century, after which the method was replaced by steel construction. SoHo bloomed as the center of New York's most elegant department stores, then entered a long period of decline with no new development, so the old buildings remained intact. These circumstances, coupled with the preservation movement of the 1970s and current restoration and renovation efforts, make SoHo one of New York's most architecturally dazzling neighborhoods.

The most visible use of cast iron is in the historically styled building facades, with their urns, festoons, finials, and stately columns. The patterns were first carved in wood, then impressed in wet or "green" sand, into which molten iron was poured. The fanciful pre-cast pieces, in Victorian Gothic, Greek Revival, Italianate, French Second Empire, Romanesque, and Queen Anne styles, could be ordered ready-made from "Badger's Illustrated Catalogue of Cast-Iron Architecture" of 1865, for example, which has been recently reprinted.

101 Spring Street

Cast iron was also used for the internal supports of the buildings, because it could bear a great load without the bulkiness of stone walls. As a result, the buildings became slimmer, taller, more spacious and airy. Magically, street floors were transformed into wide panes of glass interspersed with tall, slender iron columns that actually held up the building. The wide windows were perfect for the display of commercial goods, of course; the term "window shopping" came into vogue at this time.

In many ways, SoHo's buildings were forerunners of modern architecture in America. Historically, rich facade decoration was a sign of status, because of the time and work involved in producing it. Cast iron changed that, because ornamentation could be mass-produced inexpensively. As a result, a new aesthetic developed that was key to twentieth-century architecture: modularity. The cast-iron facades are so expressive not because they imitate past styles, but because of the regularity of their evenly spaced bays, or window groupings. This patterning of repeated, modularly produced units was the direct precursor to the skyscraper aesthetic, as you can tell just by gazing up from the low roofs of SoHo to the gleaming tower of the Empire State Building. The fact that buildings more than a century old can be put to such contemporary uses as restaurants, bars, and stores with minimal structural change shows how truly modern they are in spirit.

Steve Kahn, who has been making images as a commercial photographer and fine artist since 1969, is sensitive to the layers of experience in the daily life of the neighborhood where he has lived since 1987. His photos capture the collision of old and new—the rainbow splash of graffiti paint on a weathered cast-iron surface, the glamorous, after-hours neon glow on a building designed to look like a Roman palazzo.

97 Greene Street

SoHo is a neighborhood of passing moments, superimposed one upon another. Kahn captures quiet moments, when the light bounces off a window and illuminates some hidden corner, or the sun profiles a water tower in a shadow on a brick wall. Each generation of New Yorkers has its moment in the sunshine: like a Valkyrie on wheels, a Rollerblader swoops past an art opening by the English artists Gilbert and George. In another image, a film crew, setting up its nighttime sun to turn a city street into a stage set, look like transient spirits against the backdrop of the city. The past is always close to the surface. Today you might see a businessman chatting on a cellular phone while standing on a fire escape originally built to protect sweatshop workers. Extra-wide sidewalks that once covered underground vaults now accommodate outdoor cafes. The round glass plugs in the sidewalks once served as vault lights, letting daylight into the underground spaces used for work and storage. Steve Kahn focuses on details of decorative seals bearing street addresses and the cast-iron foundry trademarks, which look like signatures from another time.

Walking down a SoHo street is an experience in bricolage—a postmodern collage of odds and ends from all time periods, which combine to form new patterns and meanings. Kahn, who carries his camera whenever he steps out of his loft, captures these juxtapositions: a seated Buddha bathed in the same mellow light as a solitary headless mannequin, both framed by ornate cast-iron pilasters, or a gleaming car hood reflecting century-old architecture. In certain moments, SoHo still looks much as it did just after the Civil War, with its modestly scaled buildings, cobblestone streets, and cast-iron bishop's crook lampposts. From a photographer's point of view, Kahn says, SoHo is especially interesting because the buildings are low enough that nearly every surface is touched by sunlight, fleetingly illuminating details.

468 West Broadway

Kahn uses color to highlight and enliven the evanescent in this backdrop of the past: a woman smokes pensively in an ochre-walled trattoria; gold lettering glistens on a vintage bakery window; rows of brightly colored wigs shine like beakers of chemicals; and a fashion display is subordinated to the momentary pattern of light and shadow on a window gate, made solid and more permanent by the camera's eye. Kahn aims to make the reader experience SoHo freshly, by showing how the past presses through the surface like an embossment, and by demonstrating how light preserves an instant in time.

Eric Nash
New York, January 1999

ARCHITECTURE

In SoHo individual buildings are less important than the aggregate, an unparalleled grouping of urban commercial structures created from the 1850s to the 1890s, when the area around lower Broadway was the mercantile heart of New York. Focus on details: bold Tuscan columns and delicate Corinthian pilasters; the thick glass disks called vault lights set into sidewalks to illuminate basements; the name of merchant prince Charles Broadway Rouss inscribed on a lintel above the plate-glass windows of his former emporium. Step back to drink in the overall effect: afternoon sun raking cast-iron-column facades on Greene Street, or the warm lights of Prince Street shops and West Broadway bistros on a winter evening.

The SoHo Cast-Iron Historic District, designated a local historic district in 1973 and a national historic district in 1978, is twenty-six blocks bounded by Houston Street on the north (hence the name: *So*uth of *Ho*uston), Canal and Howard Streets on the south, Crosby Street on the east, and West Broadway. The district, said the report that designated it, contains "the largest concentration of full and partial cast-iron facades anywhere in the world."

James Bogardus is credited with building the first complete iron-front structure in 1848, a major advance in the development of prefabricated construction. Elegant columns inside SoHo structures illustrate iron's prime characteristic as a building material: strength in compression. Iron permitted huge plate glass windows to be set into the wide openings between a facade's attached columns, revealing the latest merchandise within.

The last iron-front building went up in 1901 (an Italianate design at 550 Broadway), completing a cycle of styles that began with the Italianate of the 1850s (488 Broadway) and continued in the 1870s and 1880s with the French Second Empire style (72–76 Greene Street) and the Neo-Grec (480 Broadway, designed by Richard Morris Hunt). Other exemplary buildings include Ernest Flagg's "Little Singer Building" at 561 Broadway, a confection of wrought iron and terra cotta. A walk up Greene Street from Canal or along Broome Street from Mercer to Wooster will provide some of the most rewarding views of cast-iron SoHo as a unique urban environment.

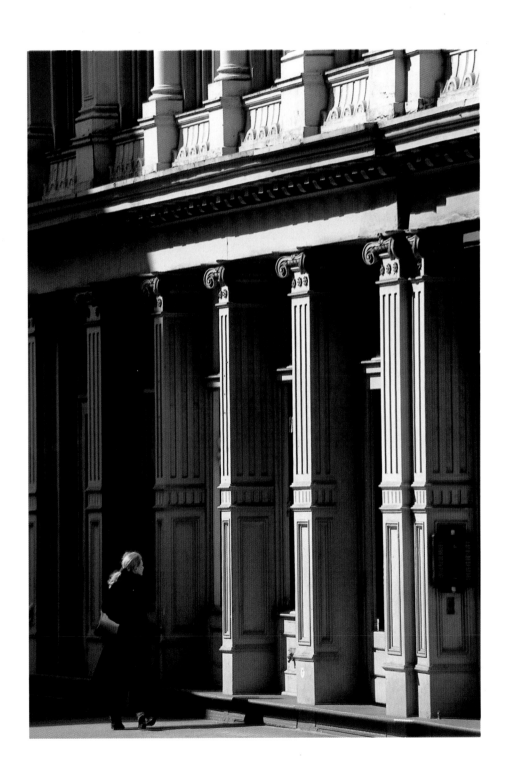

THE ARTS

If the gravitational center of New York's gallery scene has shifted to Chelsea in recent years, it's certain that the art world's heart remains in SoHo. SoHo is where you go to sniff the nostalgic perfume—part patchouli oil, part honest sweat—of a time when artists in New York were ignored, embattled, and full of conviction, carving out of looming loft buildings what became the world's preeminent center for contemporary art.

As early as the 1940s, a handful of artists had studios in the area that is now called SoHo. By the middle 1960s, as painting and sculpture began to take a back seat to installation and performance art, many artists had moved into the area, attracted by large lofts in which they could both work and live. Loft living was illegal—the area was zoned for commercial use and light manufacturing—but in the late 1960s, laws were changed to permit "artists in residence" to occupy industrial spaces in SoHo.

Paula Cooper opened the first gallery in SoHo in 1968, on Prince Street. Ivan Karp, a former director of the Leo Castelli Gallery, opened O.K. Harris Gallery on West Broadway in 1969. In 1970 Holly Solomon rented a studio at 98 Greene Street; the artist Gordon Matta-Clark built it for her. Castelli opened a downtown branch of his gallery in 1971 at 420 West Broadway, a building that eventually housed five galleries and became one of the prime gallery venues in New York. Not all of his artists were thrilled. Roy Lichtenstein, recalled Castelli, "told me that nobody will ever go there."

Today, a single block of lower Broadway features three of New York's most consistently rewarding museums: The New Museum of Contemporary Art, the Guggenheim SoHo, and the Museum for African Art. Also in SoHo is the Drawing Center on Wooster, with its meticulous shows of works on paper, and Thread Waxing Space, which hosts performance. Many prestigious galleries remain, including reliable venues such as Peter Blum, Deitch Projects, Dorsky Gallery, Gagosian Gallery, Sean Kelly Gallery, Monique Knowlton, Lehmann Maupin, PaceWildenstein, and David Zwirner. Past the milling crowds, a step beyond the sidewalk and perhaps a brief elevator ride will still bring you to a quiet space where some of the most advanced art of the day offers a rewarding respite.

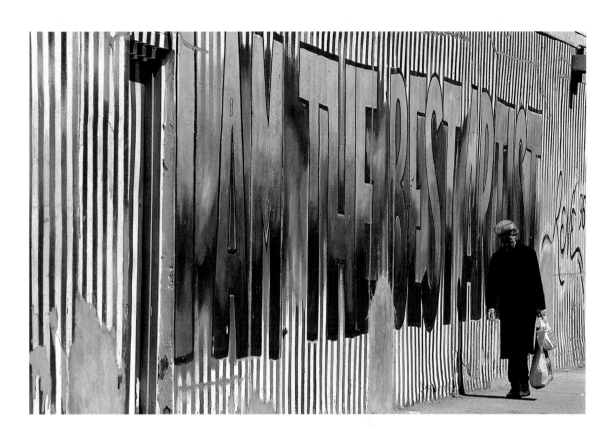

SHOPPING

Art and commerce converge in SoHo. No longer a haven for artists seeking affordable living and working spaces, it remains an environment where artistry thrives. SoHo's retailers prize originality, and one-of-a-kind merchandise and creative window displays are prevalent. The area's blend of art and economic success recalls two of SoHo's previous incarnations—as a neighborhood of artists and a shopping destination—that inform the SoHo of today.

In the 1860s Broadway was a chic address for international hotels like the St. Nicholas and the Metropolitan, and prominent department stores such as Tiffany and Co. and Haughwout's. Lord and Taylor's sumptuous Grand Street store epitomized the extravagance of the time. The white marble building was so ornate that the *New York Times* declared it "more like an Italian palace than a place for the sale of broadcloth." Yet, by the turn of the century most retail establishments had followed the population shift northward, and the elegant buildings were soon occupied by manufacturers.

SoHo's economic rebound began in the late 1960s, as the area began to draw visitors to its art galleries. Restaurants and stores soon opened, and loft buildings were converted to residences. By the late 1970s retail was booming; although Broadway is now dominated by chain stores such as Old Navy and Staples, the side streets are lined with the boutiques, specialty shops, and cafés that give the area its unique flavor. In the spirit of SoHo's numerous galleries, many stores hang clothing on the walls like art and display home furnishings as though they were sculpture.

The artists' legacy is also manifest in the bookstores of SoHo. Printed Matter, Inc., a not-for-profit organization started in 1976, sells books made by artists. The petite Untitled offers a wealth of art postcards, and Rizzoli Bookstore has a broad selection of art and architecture books.

The streets of SoHo have become a marketplace in their own right. Vendors line certain streets with tables of prints and photographs, handmade jewelry, and souvenirs. Flea markets thrive at the corners of Spring and Wooster, and, on weekends, at an outdoor parking lot stretching between Broadway and Mercer—the former site of Lord and Taylor.

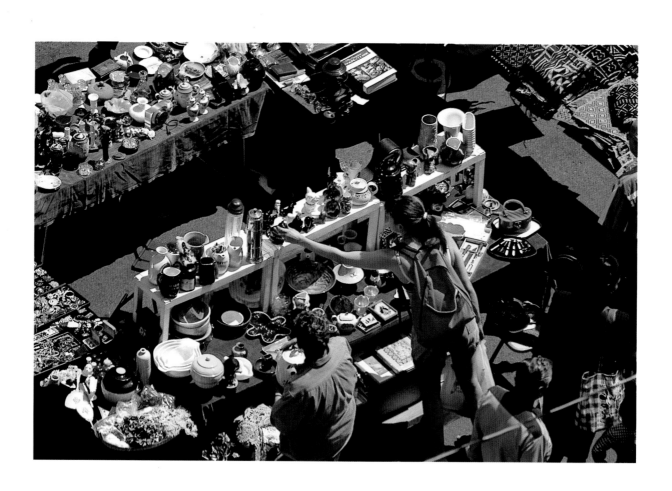

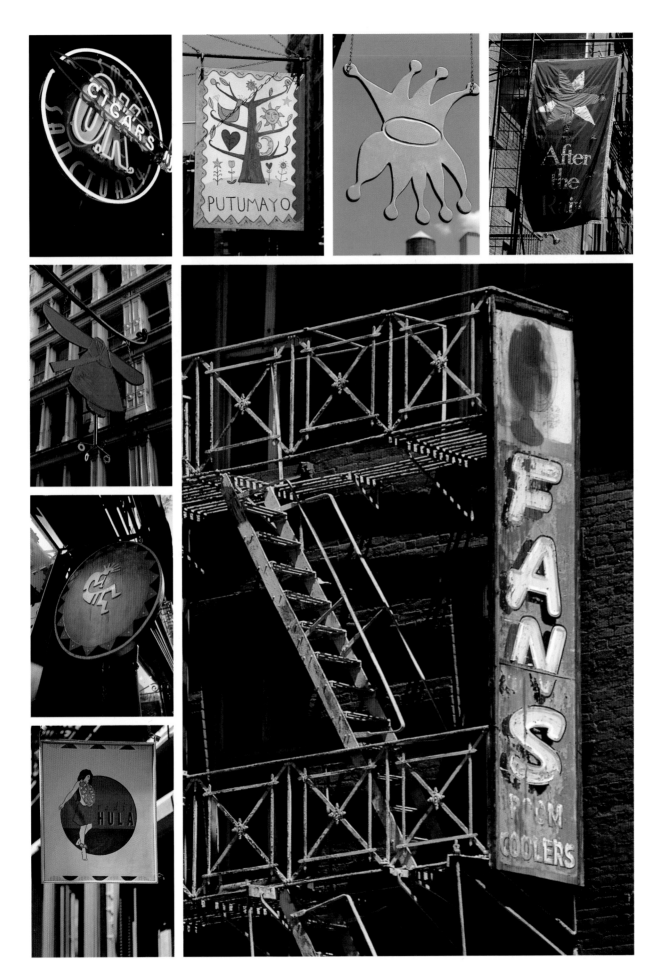

DINING

SoHo has always been about seeing and being seen. From the moment artists, art dealers, and New York's avant-garde discovered the light-filled industrial frontier south of Houston Street, the area became a destination for uptown collectors and others who wanted to see the latest art and galleries, and be seen on the new cutting edge. Today an international array of restaurants, bars, and cafés offers countless temptations—and a canvas primed for people watching, celebrity sightings, and rendezvous.

Fanelli's Café, on the corner of Prince and Mercer, began as a "grocery" in 1872 and is the second longest-running food establishment in the city. It survived Prohibition as a speakeasy and is a favorite gathering place for locals today. Other early pioneers are long gone—Food, an artists' refuge, and the cafeteria-style Kast disappeared in the seventies; Spring Street Bar offered the area's first fine dining; and Giorgio DeLuca's cheese shop has transformed into the gourmet provisioner Dean & DeLuca, which helped jump-start SoHo's food culture.

For elegant cocktails, lounge at the Merc Bar, or Pravda for blini, caviar, and, of course, vodka—or have a wine-tasting at SoHo Kitchen and Bar. Late-night restaurants—including Blue Ribbon, Café Noir, and the sublimely Parisian Balthazar—attract a young, fast-moving crowd. For those who like to linger over the morning paper, or watch the world go by, there are charming cafés and coffee shops: Once Upon a Tart, the French bistro Felix, and the lively Café Bari.

Painters and sculptors are not the only kind of artist in SoHo, as some of the country's best chefs have arrived on the scene. Katy Sparks of Quilty's and David Wurth of Savoy serve contemporary, seasonal American food in cozy, simple rooms. Alison Price's Alison on Dominick Street is a romantic, out-of-the-way gem; and for sky's-the-limit gourmets, the highly lauded Jean-Georges Vongerichten serves French-American cuisine at The Mercer Kitchen. If there is one common thread in the bustling chic of SoHo, it is this: no matter what your choice in food, fashion, art, and culture, you are part of the scene—the seeing and being seen—that is the history, the edgy excitement of SoHo.

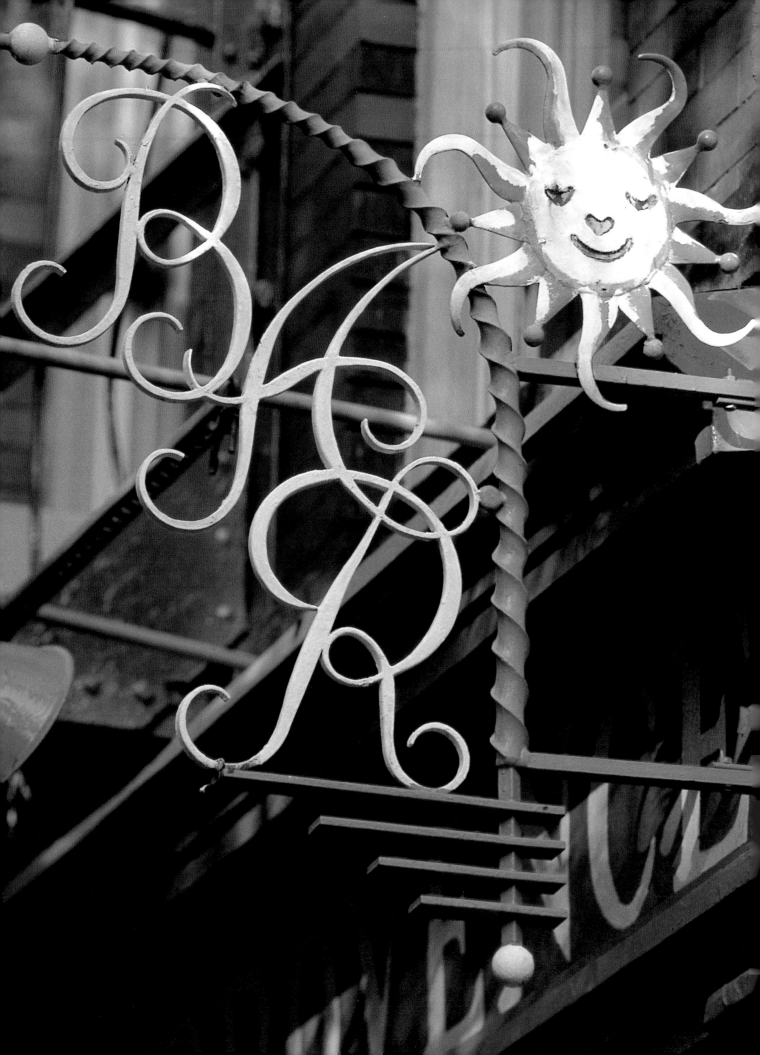

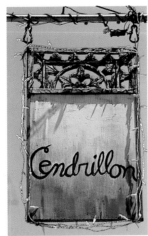

Mediterranean

PENNE with fresh tomato & basil
FUSILLI with wild mushrooms
PENNE with asparagus, parmesa
RAVIOLI with goat cheese & roaste
FUSILLI with spicy tomato sau
THIN CRUST PIZZA
SALAD NIÇOISE
GRILLED CHICKEN SAND
CROQUE MONSIEUR
TURKEY BURGER 7.50
HAMBURGER 7.50 with d
VEGETARIAN BURGER